Homophones for Kids

Little Language Lovers Series

by Erin Jacobs

Library of Congress Control Number: 2014944778

ISBN 978-1-941317-08-2

Published by Joyful Nook, an imprint of Wise Dove Group LLC 888-449-7706 | Pubs@JoyfulNook.com

Joyful Nook

Books That Make Happy Learners

Hare~Hair
Hear~Here
Ate~Eight
Air~ Heir
Days~Daze
Hay~Hey
Whine~Wine
Brake~Break
Him~Hymn
Hear~Here
Ate~Eight
Pear~Pair
Weak~Week
Brake~Break
Hay~Hey
Be~Bee
Deer~Dear
Air~ Heir
There~Their~They're
Hi~High
Weak~Week
Brake~Break
Hi~High
Hay~Hey
Pear~Pair
Be~Bee
Ate~Eight
Whine~Wine
Pear~Pair
Hi~High
Deer~Dear
Hi~High
Be~Bee
Hare~Hair
Deer~Dear
Days~Daze
Hay~Hey
Hare~Hair
Hay~Hey

This book will reveal definitions of common homophones, and how to distinguish between them.

Air- Heir
Ate- Eight
Be-Bee
Brake- Break
Deer- Dear
Days- Daze
Hear- Here
Him- Hymn
Hay- Hey
Hi- High
Hare- Hair
Pear- Pair
There- Their- They're
Weak-Week
Weather-Whether

Homophones sound alike but have different definitions. Let's practice some sentences and be word technicians.

Air - Heir

An heir is a person who will inherit a throne.

Air is what you breathe into a trombone.

The heir went outside to get some fresh air.

Ate- Eight

Eight is the number that comes after seven.

If you ate something good, then you'll feel like heaven.

Did you see Kevin? He ate eight pieces of pizza!

Be- Bee

Be means to exist, to live, or remain.

A bee is an insect that's difficult to tame.

Be careful because there are bees outside.

Brake-Break

Brakes are what stop
a car. Break is what
happens when you
throw glass quite far.

Break also means to
relax where you are.

I don't want to drive anymore.

Let's take a break before you
break the brakes.

Deer-Dear

Dear is what you call
someone you love.

A deer is an animal
that's humble like a
dove.

Oh dear, look at that deer!

Days- Daze

Days go from light to night, while daze means to feel confused, like after a fight.

I hit my head, and I've been in a daze for days.

Hear- Here

Hear is what you do with your ear.

Here tells the location of something far or near.

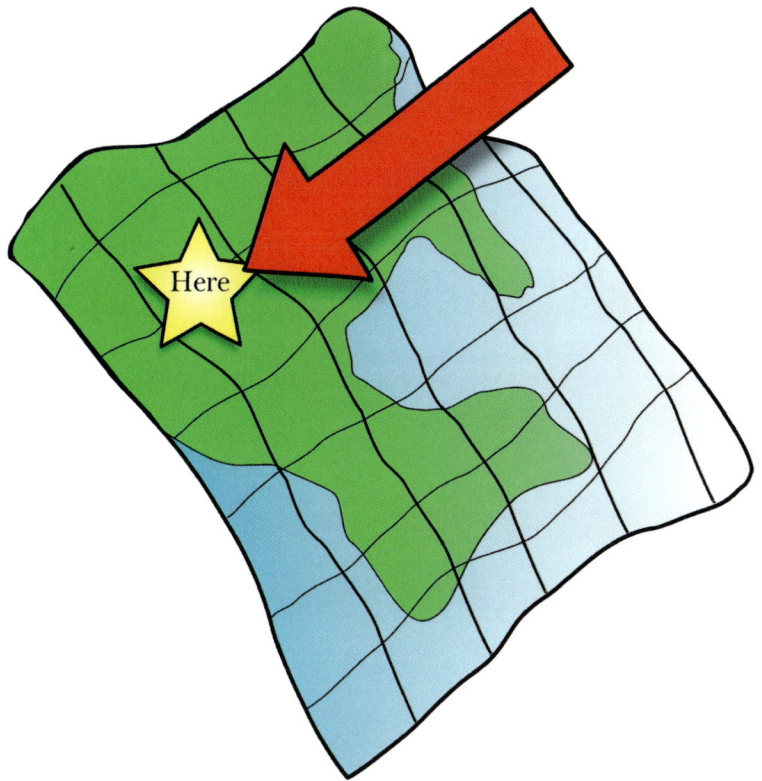

I hear that you are coming here soon.

Him-Hymn

A hymn is a song you sing in praise.

Him means "he", so don't get lost in the maze.

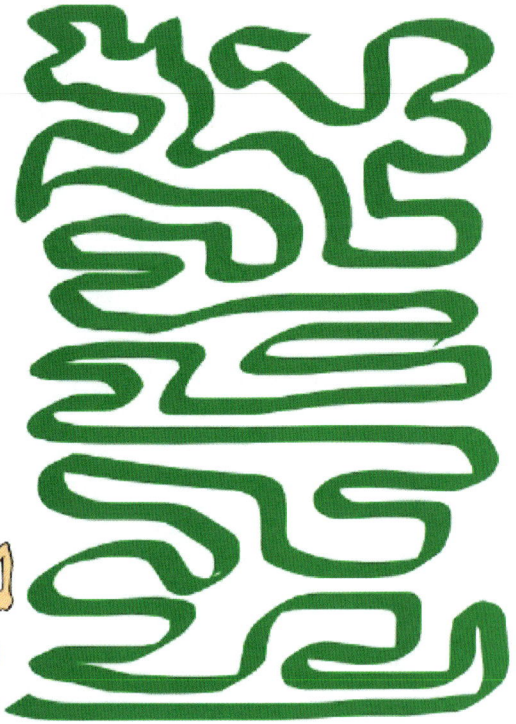

Did you hear him singing that hymn?

Hay- Hey

Hey is what you say
when you mean "stop"
or "hello".

Hay is what a horse
eats, didn't you know?

Hey, put down that hay!

Hi- High

High means high like up in the sky.

Hi means hi like the opposite of bye.

Hi, can you tell me how high this plane flies?

Hare-Hair

Hair is what you comb every day.

A hare is an animal that likes to run away.

Look at the hair on that hare!

Pear-Pair

A pair is a group of two.

A pear is a fruit- woo hoo!

Can you hand me that pair of pears?

There- Their- They're

They're means "they are" - it's a contraction.

There refers to a place; where you can see some action.

Their indicates possession.

You can get this right if you review this lesson.

They're going to handle their business over there.

Right- Write

Right means correct, or a direction.

You write with a pen, hopefully with perfection.

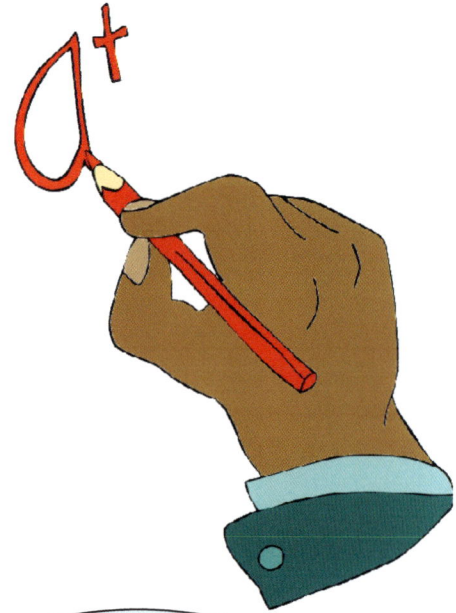

That's right, I want you to hand me the pen right there so I can write my paper.

Weak- Week

A week is seven days.

Weak is what you feel when you've been working all kind of ways.

I'm feeling weak because I've been working hard all week.

Weather- Whether

Weather refers to the atmosphere; is it rainy or sunny, or are the clouds near?

Whether is often used to introduce a question. Like whether or not you'd like to attend a session.

I wonder whether the weather will be hot or cold.

Now it's time to say goodbye. I hope these homophones haven't made you cry.

Remember- homophones are words that sound alike, but have different definitions.

Practice a few times, and you'll be in a good position.

Parts of Speech For Kids

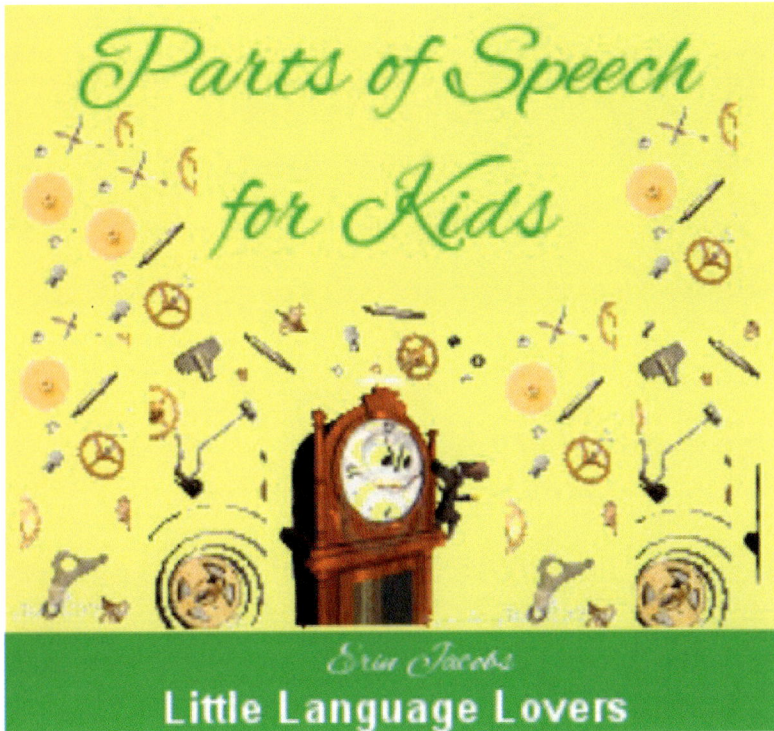

Read it once or twice, and remember the concepts for life.

Learning the parts of speech can be easy and fun with this rhyming book that teaches the basics of nouns, verbs, adjectives, adverbs, pronouns, prepositions, conjunctions, and interjections.

Visit LittleLanguageLovers.com for more information on this book and others in the series.

Parents, teachers, and grandparents- Are you ready for more learning fun? To receive updates on future books in this series and other educational children's books, please join our private email list at
http://www.JoyfulNook.com/HM

About the Author

Erin Jacobs is a mother, writer, and ESL teacher who enjoys making learning fun for her children and students. You can learn more about her Little Language Lovers book series at www.LittleLanguageLovers.com

Printed in Poland
by Amazon Fulfillment
Poland Sp. z o.o., Wrocław